D0626122

# MEGA BOOK OF

# TRUCKS

INTERNET
LINKED

96242

FREIGHTLINER

P211503

CHRYSALIS CHILDREN'S BOOKS

# INTERNET SAFETY

Always follow these guidelines for a fun and safe
journey through cyberspace:

1. Ask your parents for permission before you go online.

2. Spend time with your parents online
and show them your favourite sites.

3. Post your family's e-mail address, even if you have your
own (only give your personal address to someone you trust).

4. Do not reply to e-mails if you feel
they are strange or upsetting.

5. Do not use your real surname while you are online.

6. Never arrange to meet 'cyber friends' in person
without your parents' permission.

7. Never give out your password.

8. Never give out your home address or telephone number.

9. Do not send scanned pictures of yourself
unless your parents approve.

10. Leave a website straight away if you find something that
is offensive or upsetting. Talk to your parents about it.

Every effort has been made to ensure none of the recommended websites in this book is linked to inappropriate material. However, due to the ever-changing nature of the Internet, the publishers regret they cannot take responsibility for future content of these websites. Therefore, it is strongly advised that children and parents consider the safety guidelines above.

First published in the UK in 2002 by Chrysalis Children's Books PLC
The Chrysalis Building, Bramley Road, London, W10 6SP

Copyright © Chrysalis Children's Books

A ZIGZAG BOOK

ISBN 1 904516 21 1

British Library Cataloguing in Publication Data for this book is available from the British Library.

Author: Lynne Gibbs
Editorial Director: Honor Head
Art Director: Simon Rosenheim
Senior Editor: Rasha Elsaeed
Picture Researcher: Jenny Barlow
Assistant Editor: Clare Chambers
Assistant Designer: Keren-Orr Greenfeld

Printed and bound in Hong Kong

# CONTENTS

The fuel-driven truck is a wonder of modern motoring. We rely on trucks to do many different tasks. They remove our waste, deliver food to supermarkets, transport goods to countries all over the world and play a vital role in our emergency services. This book takes a closer look at the history of these transport machines and the role they play in today's world.

**MEGA FACT**

*A truck, also called a lorry, is a motor vehicle that carries freight (goods or load). Because of their flexibility and speed, trucks now carry a quarter of all internal freight in the United States.*

*Trucks are classified as either straight or articulated. On a 'straight truck', axles are attached to a single frame. An articulated vehicle has two or more separate frames connected by couplings.*

## RISE OF THE LONG-HAUL TRUCK

As demand for bigger, more powerful engines grew, manufacturers like Mercedes-Benz, Cummins and Scania, turned to V8 engines. These have between 4 and 16 cylinders and the advantage of more compact dimensions than in-line units. In 2000, Scania launched its R164 long haulage truck with the latest, powerful, 16-litre V8 engine.

*Power is transmitted through a clutch, gearbox and differential drive. Most gearboxes have a mainshaft and twin countershafts. Many modern trucks are now automatic.*

*Modern trucks have electronically controlled front and rear disc brakes. Brakes usually actuated by compressed air through a system of valves. By law, all trucks must have an independent secondary system of brakes.*

*Some axles have the secondary reduction gearing in the wheel hubs, reducing drive-shaft stress and allowing a smaller differential housing which gives improved ground clearance. The drive from the gearbox to the rear axle is transmitted by a propeller shaft with universal joints.*

## PETROL VERSUS DIESEL

Until the 1930s, the petrol engine was widely used for trucks, especially in the United States. Since World War II, diesel-powered engines, such as the Scania L-Class, have become more popular for trucks used on heavy, long-distance hauls (transport). Diesel trucks are often more costly than similar models using petrol-burning engines, but they are more efficient burners of fuel.

Early road transport depended on the horse-drawn cart. The first steam-powered vehicle was built in 1769 by French military engineer, Nicholas Joseph Cugnot. His three-wheeled steam machine ran for fifteen minutes at about 10 km/h. The vehicle was driven through the front wheel and the weight of the mechanisms made it difficult to steer. In 1803, Richard Trevithick produced a steam carriage to transport passengers from Leather Lane to Paddington in London.

## THORNYCROFT

Designed in 1864, the Thornycroft steam-powered van wasn't built until 1896. With a one-tonne payload the van was displayed at the 1898 Crystal Palace Show in London, England. Thornycroft's steam-powered traction engines had also been used to pull loads and to drive machinery. As one of the world's first load-bearing, commercial vehicles, it is closest form of transport to the modern truck.

**MEGA FACT**
*Gottlieb Daimler in Germany built the first motor truck in 1896. It was equipped with an four-horsepower engine and a belt drive with two speeds forward. In 1898, the Winton Company in the USA produced a petrol-powered delivery wagon, with a single-cylinder, six-horsepower engine.*

**MEGA FACT**
*Cugnot's steam artillary tractor of 1770 was acknowledged as the world's first self-propelled road vehicle.*

# LACRE MOTOR CAR

The Lacre Motor Car Company began producing cars and light vans in 1902. From 1909, Lacre, which derived its name from an abbreviation of Long Acre in London, where it was based, began producing trucks up to 9 tonnes payload capacity. During World War I, Lacre focused on building military vehicles. After the war, the company switched to manufacturing road sweepers. Load-carrying trucks continued to be produced until the company wound up in 1928.

In 1907, the upmarket Harrods store in Brompton Road, London, used this early Lacre van to deliver goods to their wealthy customers. Trucks now had air suspension and electric lighting instead of paraffin and acetylene. Bigger, heavier trucks also had pneumatic tyres, which made for a more comfortable ride.

# THE FIRST LEYLAND VAN

Leyland began in 1896 when James Sumner and the Spurrier family founded the Lancashire Steam Motor Company in the town of Leyland, in north-west England. In the same year, with the help of 20 employees, Sumner completed his first vehicle – a 1.5-tonne-capacity steam wagon, with oil-fired boiler, cart wheels and tiller steering. It was the start of what was to become an unbeaten heritage of engineering and outstanding production performance that has made today's Leyland trucks popular.

**MEGA FACT**
*Although pneumatic tyres appeared on vehicles as early as 1904, large trucks still used hard rubber tyres until World War I. Cotton was replaced by synthetics in the carcass of truck tyres in the 1930s, with steel wire and fibreglass plies appearing later.*

*'Pig' was the name given to Leyland's first petrol-engined truck. An improved model appeared in 1905, with production reaching 16 chassis.*

**MEGA FACT**
*The diesel engine was first demonstrated by German engineer Rudolph Diesel in 1897.*

**MEGA FACT**
*In 1955, tubeless tyres became available in large truck sizes.*

# ALBION

Founded in 1899, the Albion Motor Car Company produced its first commercial vehicle, a half-tonne van, in 1902. In 1910, Albion produced their A10 truck for three to four-tonne payloads. This had a four-cylinder petrol engine and chain drive. Albion built six thousand of these trucks for service in World War 1. The company also supplied military trucks during World War II, producing three-tonne 4x4s, 10-tonne 6x4s and heavy-duty tank transporters. In 1951, Albion was taken over by Leyland Motors, and most of Albion's heavy trucks were phased out.

**INTERNET LINK**
www.logisticsworld
.co.uk
Check out this website to get some great trucking info and downloads of your favourite truck pictures.

# FODEN

Foden Limited started life when Hancock and Foden began building agricultural machinery and steam engines in 1856. In 1887, Edwin Foden demonstrated a prototype (first model) steam traction engine.

By 1901, Foden's steam truck was cruising at 10 km/h. The company reluctantly stopped producing steam trucks in 1934 due to the popularity of internal-combustion-engined trucks.

# BIG RIGS

Big rigs, such as Freightliners, are among the most powerful trucks. Trains for these trucks can weigh between 500 to 1000 tonnes, and up to four tractors can be coupled together to provide the tractive effort. Tractors are powered by turbo-charged and after-cooled diesel engines and can weigh up to 40 tonnes each.

**INTERNET LINK**

http://www.ford-trucks.com
Get the latest information about your favourite Ford trucks. You can click on to other miscellaneous websites from here to learn more about monster, offroad, racing, classic and antique trucks.

*The lack of roads and waterways encouraged the Australians to create the monster-long 'road train'. This solved the problem of transporting supplies across the country.*

# SCANIA HEAVY ARTIC

With its new cab design and low-emission diesel powers, this R144 articulated truck from Scania's model 4 series has a 14-litre engine capacity. The prefix 'R' indicates a full-height cab (as this picture shows), 'P' indicates a low-profile cab and 'T' a bonneted cab. Celebrating its centenary in 1991, it took Scania 75 years to build its first 1000,000 vehicles. Vehicle number 500,000 was made in 1987 – 96 years after the company was founded. But it took just 13 years to build the next half million – by the year 2000!

# AUSSIE ROAD TRAIN

These trucks are only found in Australia and were originally produced to service far-flung communities. Around five percent of the total transportation in Australia takes place via road trains. Rigs have huge trailer combinations measuring up to 53 metres in length. Rigs carry around 140 tonnes each – equivalent to 400 head of cattle or 125,000 litres of aviation fuel. Scania's 480 and 580 hp 16-litre V8 engines are capable of high average speeds at modest fuel consumption. The Scania 470 hp 12-litre turbo-compound engine is another truck often used for road-train deliveries in the outback.

# MONSTER TRUCKS

The Monster truck was born when a few enthusiasts in the 1970s began making their pickups bigger and better by adding huge tyres and faster engines. The first Monster truck is Bigfoot, built from a Ford F250 pick-up truck. In the early 1980s, chrome-crunching monsters appeared at motor sports events and fairs, where they were rolled over cars with the sole intention of flattening them. By the mid-1980s, car crushing gave way to race-style competitions.

### BIGGER AND BETTER

Coil over and nitrogen charged suspension systems, huge 170-centimetre tall tyres and alcohol-injected engines generate over 1,500 horsepower, making today's monster trucks bigger, tougher and meaner than ever.

# MONSTER ROLLOVER

Overkill, from Fort Wayne, Indiana, USA, is one of the lightest trucks on the American circuits. The MTRA (Monster Truck Racing Association) state that all racing monster trucks must weigh a minimum 4500 kilograms. For Overkill, which weighs 90 kilograms under the limit, to keep its tyres on the ground, weights have to be added to it.

## MEGA WEIRD

*Monster trucks are built for short, high-powered bursts of speed. They generate an average of 1,500 to 2,000 horsepower and are capable of up to 160 kilometres per hour. These huge trucks can jump 35-38 metres (more than 14 cars side by side) and up to eight metres in the air.*

## MEGA FACT

*Built in 1991, Snake Bite competed in the USA on the PENDA points series until 1994. The latest model, a 1997 Ford, has a 572ci Ford Hemi engine, a GTS fibreglass body and a custom nose. Its flashing eyes and snake fangs are highlighted by a custom 'scaled' paint scheme. Snake Bite was the first Monster Truck to be retro-fitted with a fibreglass body .*

# CAROLINA CRUSHER

The first Carolina Crusher was built in North Carolina, USA, in 1985. Since then, these 'monsters' have been improved with each successive model. Some of the older Carolina Crusher's were sold to English promoters, and now have new names. One is called the Bandit, and tours across the United Kingdom.

## MEGA MILITARY
*The first side-by-side monster truck race took place in 1992. Instead of racing against the clock, these huge beasts raced head to head!*

# PURE ADRENALIN

The chassis on this 2000 Ford Super Duty truck was especially built to accommodate the John Hutcherson Custom Turbo 400 Transmission and 557 cubic inch Fontana Hemi engine. Weighing 4672 kilograms, this up-to-the-minute monster made its debut in April 2000, entering the first pro MT (professional MonsterTruck) race in South Carolina, USA. In 2001, Pure Adrenalin went on to take third place in the pro MT race series, competing against such fearsome foes as Bigfoot.

## INTERNET LINK
http://www.robosaurus.co]
http://www.monstertruckracing.com
http://www.bigfoot4x4.com
There is even more Monster Truck info here!

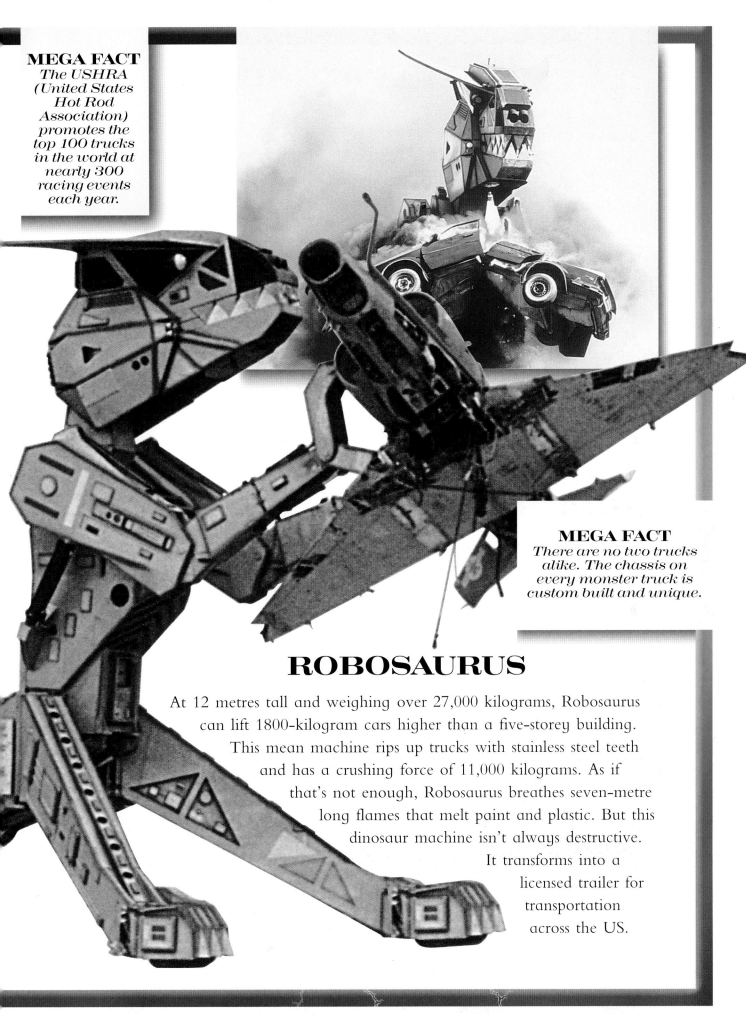

# ROBOSAURUS

At 12 metres tall and weighing over 27,000 kilograms, Robosaurus can lift 1800-kilogram cars higher than a five-storey building. This mean machine rips up trucks with stainless steel teeth and has a crushing force of 11,000 kilograms. As if that's not enough, Robosaurus breathes seven-metre long flames that melt paint and plastic. But this dinosaur machine isn't always destructive. It transforms into a licensed trailer for transportation across the US.

# SPECIALISED TRUCKS

Basic truck bodies can only be adapted up to a limit. This is why purpose-built models are needed for many tasks for which trucks are used today. These jobs include transporting load, such as timber logs and hazardous chemicals, putting out fires and lifting heavy objects. Specialised trucks are designed to cope with almost every kind of job.

**MEGA FACT**
*The first bus service in Britain was started in Manchester in 1824, by John Greenwood. It ran from Pendleton to Manchester.*

### TWO FOR ONE

Caterpillar grew from the 1925 merger of two American agricultural equipment manufactures, Holt Manufacturing Company and the C L Best Gas Traction Company.

### GOOD SOLUTION

Benjamin Holt produced agricultural equipment, such as combine harvesters that used steam-traction engines to pull them through the fields. These heavy engines often sank into the ground. In 1904, Holt tested the first practical crawler tractor. He removed the rear drive wheels from a Holt Junior Road Engine and replaced them with a pair of tracks, three metres long and 60 centimetres wide.

### INTERNET LINK

http://www.pcgame.com
Find cheats, tips and short-cuts for some of the latest truck-racing games. Lots of free downloads for Formula 1, NASCAR, Off-Road, Kart and Monster truck games, too.

# TRUCK FEST

Truck Fest is Europe's biggest truck show, an annual meeting event for the Road Haulage Industry, as well as buyers and enthusiasts. Highlights include stunt action from the best Monster Trucks, and competitions to find the best new truck, the best working truck, the best vintage truck and even best paintwork.

# ARMOURED

Trucks play a major part in military operations all over the world and have been used by the armed forces since World War I. Oshkosh Truck Corporation is one of the leading manufacturers of specialised military trucks. Protected from gunfire and even landmines, armoured trucks are now able to go into more dangerous areas that were often avoided.

**MEGA WEIRD**
*Armies carry equipment in amphibious trucks that are able to drive on land and float on water. To stop water flooding the engine, these trucks have a waterproof underside.*

# CONCRETE MIXER

Many of today's concrete mixers are 6x4s with drum capacities of six to seven cubic metres. Some larger multi-axle mixers have drum capacities of between 12 and 15 cubic metres. Modern concrete mixers, often called 'readymix' trucks, have a separate engine to turn the drum at different speeds. Some have a P T O (power take-off) which allows auxiliary equipment to be driven off the vehicle's gearbox or engine.

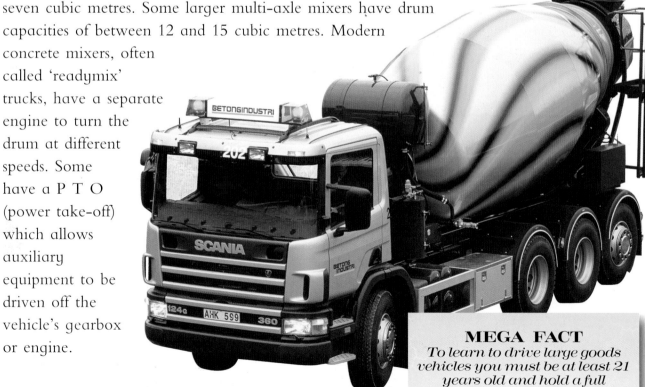

**MEGA FACT**
*To learn to drive large goods vehicles you must be at least 21 years old and hold a full standard driving licence.*

# TANKER

There are two basic types of tanker – those that carry bulk liquids and those for bulk powders. Bulk liquid tankers have been built since the early 1920s. The early vehicles had rectangular bodies. Cylindrical and elliptical barrels followed later, with better manufacturing techniques. Bulk powder tankers have only been made since the 1950s. Some tanks consist of one compartment, while others can have five or more separate compartments for different products and grades. When carrying dangerous chemicals, strict safety codes are applied and drivers must have special training.

**INTERNET LINK**

http://www.nfpa.org
There are some fun things to do – like learning about all the different parts of a fire truck.

# FIRE TRUCK

Fire trucks have advanced dramatically since open appliances with warning bells roared through our streets, with the crew clinging onto their sides. Long after most trucks began using diesel engines, fire trucks continued to use petrol, which gave faster acceleration. Scania export their fire trucks to countries all over the world. One of the reasons for Scania's success is their specially designed CrewCab for advanced emergency-rescue applications.

# RECOVERY TRUCK

Modern recovery trucks are capable of removing a vehicle weighing up to 50 tonnes. In the past, most recovery trucks used a crane jib to lift a vehicle. With engine sizes reaching 500bhp, tow trucks today are likely to come fitted with an innovative 12-tonne underlift capability. This is a powerful hydraulic boom that can be extended under the truck to support the front axle. Self-loading, lightweight trucks are still used by small garages and private users.

**MEGA FACT**
*In 1977, a Kenworth diesel truck transported the space shuttle, Enterprise, 64 kilometres across the Mojave Desert in the USA. The Kenworth was capable of pulling loads of over 500 tonnes, so the shuttle's mere 75 tonnes was a piece of cake!*

**MEGA FACT**
*Some fire trucks have telescopic ladders over 40 metres long, enabling them to reach the eleventh floor of a building.*

# LOGGING TRUCK

There are two classes of logging truck – those that operate on public roads and those restricted to private forestry areas. Only those trucks travelling on public roads have to conform to length and weight limits. Companies including Kenworth, Mack, Scania and Volvo produce huge, high-powered tractors designed specifically for the logging industry. Special trailers with bolsters are used to carry logs. Larger trucks can haul three or more trailers, each carrying around 50 tonnes.

**INTERNET LINKS**
http://www.howstuffworks.com
Click on 'automotive' to see how engines, brakes and even racing cars work!

# GARBAGE TRUCK

Gone are the days of the covered dump truck, built with just a standard chassis and a hatch through which refuse could be emptied. With the huge increase in household refuse (waste) in the last 30 to 40 years, massive three and four-axled trucks at up to 32 tonnes gvw (gross vehicle weight) are now used. These trucks have automatic transmission and the latest hydraulic compression equipment.

# MOBILE CRANE

Today, most cranes are purpose-built and highly specialised, but early mobile cranes were mounted on truck chassis. Cranes with lifting capacities from 10 to 100 tonnes are often adequate, although there are companies, such as Krupp, that produce a crane with a lifting capacity for 1000 tonnes!

# 4X4 – OFF ROAD

At one time, the only trucks to have four-wheel drive, also known as 4WD or 4x4, were 'off-road' vehicles such as Jeeps and military vehicles. These machines were designed to travel over rough, muddy terrain (land), which would be impossible for two-wheel drive vehicles. Modern 4x4 trucks are becoming popular because of their efficiency, stability on cornering and easy maneuverability. Four-wheel drive SUTs (Sports Utility Trucks), which are often seen on city roads, combine the latest technology and high-performance with stylish good looks.

## MEGA INFO

Understanding what veteran SUV enthusiasts are talking about can sometimes be confusing! Here some of the terms used to help you keep up with the jargon!

2WD = Two-Wheel Drive
4WD = Four-Wheel Drive
AWD = All-Wheel Drive
GVWR = Gross Vehicle Weight Rating
GAWR = Gross Axle Weight Rating
GCWR = Gross Combined Weight Rating

### FOUR-WHEEL

On four-wheel drive trucks, such as the Hummer, the engine makes all the wheels turn. This gives more stability when travelling at speed, especially in poor conditions, such as snow and rain.

### TWO-WHEEL DRIVE

Two-wheel drive vehicles are either 'front' wheel drive or 'rear' wheel drive. This means that only the two front wheels or back wheels move the vehicle along. If too much power is applied to these driving wheels or the road surface is slippery, then the tyres can easily lose their grip on the road surface.

# HUMMER ON ICE

The typical FWD system comprises of a gearbox, a transfer box that selects the power to either two- or four-wheel drives, and two sets of driving axles or drive shafts. On 4WDs, all four wheels can be driven all of the time, or just some of the time. There are normally two positions for 4WD: 'High 4' is used for dusty, dirt or wet roads, and 'Low 4' is used on snow, sand or mud surfaces at much slower speeds.

### MULTIPLE HUMMERS

The Hummer was originally designed as an all-purpose vehicle for the American Armed Forces, where it is known as the Humvee. The Hummer went on sale to the public in October 1992. Available in two-door Hard Top, four-door Hard Top, Open Top and Wagon, the Hummer goes from 0-95 km/h in just 16 seconds, with a top speed of around 135 km/h. A Central Tyre Inflation System now allows the driver to inflate or deflate the tyres from inside the vehicle.

**MEGA FACT**
Since 1999, the Hummer's standard traction-control system means that running soft tyres may be in the past. TorqTrac4 uses sensors on all wheels to monitor wheel slip. If wheel speed exceeds vehicle speed, the system applies braking to the spinning wheel and transfers torque to the wheels that still have some grip.

# CHRYSLER JEEP CHEROKEE

The Cherokee was introduced to British buyers in the early 1990s, when there was an increase in demand for 4x4 transport. The Grand Cherokee 4.0 Limited was launched in 1996. With full time 4WD, cruise control, central locking, air conditioning, electric windows and mirrors, heated electric front seats, twin airbags, alarm and immobiliser, this truck has practically every modern convenience you can think of.

# LAND ROVER DISCOVERY

In 1948, the first prototype Land-Rovers were built on Jeep chassis. As steel was scarce after World War II, the body was made of an aluminium alloy. Land Rover Discovery I was released in the UK in 1989 to fill the gap between the Range Rover and Land Rover Defender. It had permanent 4WD, four doors and the option of a diesel engine.

# 4X4 PICK-UP

In 1948, Ford introduced what has become one of their best-selling trucks – the Ford F150 Regular Cab Pick-Up. This sturdy, reliable vehicle was intended to meet all the demands of the work-truck user, while comfortably seating three people. The F150 SuperCab, launched in 1974, provided a larger cab with a small rear-seat area for luggage or occasional six-passenger transportation. The Ford F-Series has been the best-selling truck in the United States for more than twenty years.

# FORD EXPLORER

The Ford Explorer 4.0, a good seller in the USA, was launched in the UK in 1997. With a petrol-guzzling 4008cc engine, this 4x4 will do around 20-25mpg. The truck comes with a five-speed automatic transmission, full-time 4WD and self-levelling rear suspension.

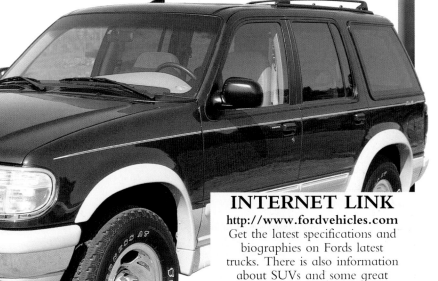

# TRUCKS BUILT FOR SPEED

Truck racing is becoming a popular spectator sport the United States and Europe. In 1994, truck racing was been split into two categories. The Super Race class is the truck equivalent of 'Formula 1' car racing. The Race Truck class involves normal commercial trucks that have been modified for racing safely. In the Super Race class, it is mainly manufacturers' teams that compete against each other, whereas the Race Class is for the private driver. The maximum speed for both race classes is 160 km/h. Each vehicle is fitted with a calibrated and sealed tachograph that makes it possible to check that the speed limit is kept.

## MEGA WEIRD

*When the first British truck racing event was held at Donington Park in 1984, access roads were blocked and the M1 motorway had a five-mile tail-back of traffic in each direction. This earned Leicestershire the record for the biggest ever traffic jam, gaining a place in the Guinness Book of Records!*

### DISQUALIFED RACERS

A turbo-plus supercharger helps to push in diesel. However, this can cause too much black smoke – which may lead to disqualification.

# HISTORY OF TRUCK RACING

Truck Racing began in the USA in 1979 at the banked super-speedway in Atlanta, Georgia. The first British event took place at Donington Park, England, in 1984. Over 80,000 spectators watched forty trucks speeding round the track. Race drivers included many professional truckers, as well as drivers from different motor sports, such as the motorcyclist Barry Sheene.

## SAFETY FIRST

A roll cage must be fitted to the inside of a cab, original seats are usually replaced with racing seats, and a fire extinguisher is compulsory. Drivers must wear fireproof overalls, a crash helmet, gloves and boots.

## INTERNET LINKS

**http://www.btra.co.uk**
Run by the British Truck Racing Association, this site has the latest news and truck racing events, and the rules and regulations.

**http://www.chrishodgetrucks.co.uk**
Click on to find out about trucking events, including racing and festivals, plus an archive of vintage trucks.

# STEVE PARRISH

The modern European Truck Championship is almost as high-tech as Formula 1 racing. The 160km/h imposed speed limit makes racing more exciting, as races are won or lost under cornering, acceleration or breaking. Racing for Mercedes-Benz, British racer Steve Parrish won 10 Championship Races between 1987 and 1996. He collected cups for five British Championships and another five for the European Championships.

## PIKES PEAK

Sharply rising 4,300-metres from the Colorado plains, Pikes Peak is visible from hundreds of kilometres away. This dangerous sprint of 20 kilometres, has 156 gravel turns and cliffs of 600 metres with no guard-rails. The Pikes Peak International Hill Climb is a race that combines a gravel course two miles above sea level, thin air and the latest technology. The race, which is televised in 56 countries, involves vehicles, including trucks of all classes, struggling to complete the arduous course. Race drivers have challenged the mountain since 1916, and it is the second oldest motor sports event in the US, after the Indianapolis 500.

# DONINGTON PARK

The BTRA (British Truck Racing Association) was formed in 1984 to organise and promote truck racing in the UK. The first UK truck race was held in 2002 at Donington Park in Derbyshire, England. It was such a success that the sport crossed the water – and European truck racing was born.

# PICKUP TRUCK RACING

Take more than 230bhp from pedigree racing engines and a tubular chassis covered in a Pickup-style glass-fibre body, and you have one of the most exciting racing categories today. The racing is fast as trucks race nose to tail. Each year, the Pickups wow bigger crowds as they feature at a host of high-profile race meetings during a 12-round season.

## INTERNET LINK
http://www.donington.co.uk
For information about forthcoming races, dates – and the machines that take part. You can even book your entrance tickets from here.

## MEGA FACT
*Truckers are allowed to drive a maximum of nine hours each day, which can be extended to ten hours on two occasions per week.*

29

# GLOSSARY

**ARTICULATED** A vehicle that is capable of bending in the middle.

**BHP** Brake Horse Power. A measurement of the engine's maximum power output.

**CARBURETTOR** Instrument for mixing fuel and air into a combustible vapour.

**CLUTCH** A device that connects and disconnects the wheels from the engine, enabling the gears to be changed.

**DISTRIBUTOR** Ignition system device on multi-cylinder engines that send the high-tension spark to the correct cylinder.

**EXHAUST** Part of an engine through which the exhausted gases or steam pass.

**MEGA FACT**
*Earthquake II is the fastest jet-powered semi truck in the world. It reaches speeds of more than 450 kilometres per hour. The engine is from a J-79-2 Phantom Fighter Plane, used on the F-4 Phantom and B-58 Hustler.*

**CRANKSHAFT** The part of the engine which changes the linear movement of the piston into rotational movement.

**HYDRAULIC** Worked by liquid. Liquid pumped to the cylinders moves pistons in or out to move a machine's parts.

IGNITION TIMING  Electrical system that produces a spark to ignite the fuel/air mixture in a petrol engine.

POWER STEERING  Designed to make the wheel move more easily than in a manual steering system.

RPM  Revolutions Per Minute – a unit of measure used to express the rotational speed of an engine.

SUSPENSION
The series of springs and dampers on the underside of a vehicle. The suspension allows the vehicle to travel more smoothly over bumps and uneven surfaces.

MARQUEE
The brand name of a truck manufacturer. Ford, Chrysler, Kenworth, Man, ERF and Bedford are well-known marques.

PNEUMATIC  Worked by air pressure, or containing air.

TRANSMISSION  A mechanism that includes the gears, linking the power produced by the engine to the drive wheels.

**MEGA WEIRD**
*Studies conducted by the University of California and Mercedes-Benz found that bright yellow and bright blue are the safest and most visible colours for vehicles.*

# INDEX

## Truck Motoring Magazines:

| | | | |
|---|---|---|---|
| Chevy Truck | Four Wheeler | OFF-ROAD | Truckin' |
| Classic Trucks | Mini Truckin' Magazine | Truck Trend Online | TRUCKWORLD™ |

## Picture Credits

L = left; R = right; T = top; B = bottom; C = centre

Front cover and 3 (see repeat use below)
4-5 Scania; 6 The British Commercial Vehicle Museum Trust; 7T Reed Business Information; 7B Company Archive, Harrods Limited; 8 The British Commercial Vehicle Museum Trust; 9T & B Reed Business Information; 10-11 & 11 Scania; 12-13 ATM Images; 13TL, TC & TR Andrew Fielder; 14T & B Andrew Fielder; 14-15 & 15T www.robosaurus.com; 16-17 courtesy of Caterpillar Inc.; 17T Truckfest; 18B Scania; 19B Scania; 20T Freightliner Trucks, a division of Freightliner LLC, Freightliner is a DaimlerChrysler company; 20B Jonathan Reeves; 21T Scania; 21B TRH Pictures; 22 ATM Images; 23B ATM Images; 24T & B ATM Images; 26-27 Caterpillar TRD; 27T Jonathan Reeves; 28T Jonathan Reeves; 28BL David Muench/Corbis; 24BR Pikes Peak International Hill Climb; 29T John Colley; 24B EMPICS; 30-31 Volvo Construction Equipment.
All other pictures Chrysalis Images